The Sticky Secret of Gecko Toes

by Rebecca L. Johnson

Table of Contents

Get Started	inside front cover
Hello, Gecko!	2
All Around and Upside Down	3
Talented Toes	4
How Does It Work?	5
Copying Mother Nature	6
Respond and Go Beyond	8
Stretch Your Brain	8
Interpret a Diagram	inside back cover

Millmark
EDUCATION

Hello, Gecko!

What's that climbing up the wall? It's a lizard!

It isn't just any lizard. It's a gecko. Nearly 1,200 different kinds of geckos live in the warm regions of the world. Some are brightly colored, while others are gray or brown. Many geckos have spots, streaks, or stripes. None of them is very large. A gecko can usually fit in the palm of your hand.

Geckos are noisy lizards. Their calls sound like "gek-oh, gek-oh." That is how geckos got their name!

Look, no lids! A gecko doesn't have eyelids. It uses its long tongue to lick its eyes clean.

Other lizards (about 3,800 kinds)

Geckos (about 1,200 kinds)

How many? There are about 5,000 different kinds of lizards in the world. About one-fourth of them are geckos.

All Around and Upside Down

Geckos can run fast. That's good because most of the insects they eat move fast, too.

To catch a meal, geckos will go anywhere. They are amazing climbers. In seconds, they can run down a tree trunk or up a wall. They can run across a ceiling and hang upside down. Geckos can even hang on to something as smooth and slippery as glass. How do they do it? The secret is in their toes.

Gotcha! **A gecko catches much of its food on the run.**

Get a grip! **A gecko can walk down a glass window without falling off.**

Connect Skills to Language

Use the photos, text, and what you already know to **draw conclusions** about geckos. How does color help geckos? How do you think geckos protect themselves?

You can use sentences like these as you draw conclusions to answer the questions:

From the photos and the text, I've learned that ____.

I already know that ____.

So, I think that ____.

Talented Toes

The bottoms, or pads, of most geckos' toes have many small ridges. The ridges are made up of tiny hairs. Each toe pad has nearly one million of these hairs.

Each hair divides, or branches, at its tip. The tip of each hair branches to form hundreds of extremely small endings. These endings grip the surface a gecko is climbing on and help the gecko hold on.

I DIDN'T KNOW THAT!

Recently scientists found the oldest known gecko **fossil**. The fossil is at least 100 million years old. The toe pads on the fossil foot look just like those of geckos today!

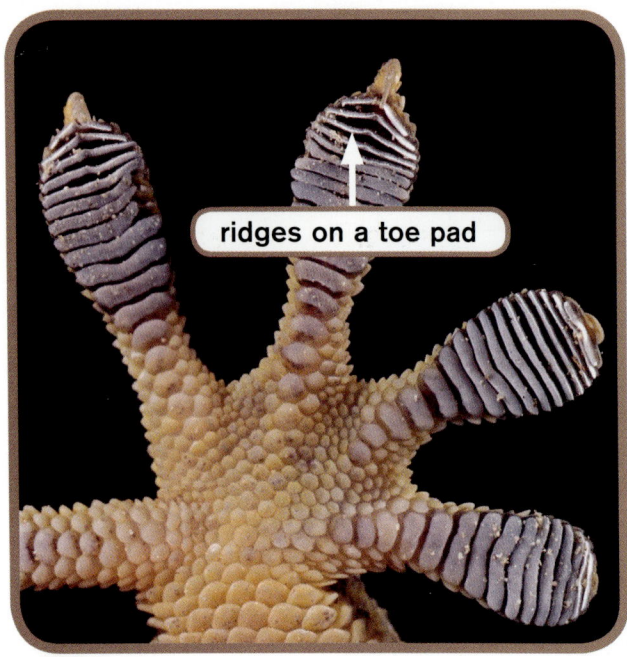

gecko toe

ridges on a toe pad

ridges of hairs

How Does It Work?

How do you think a gecko's toe pads feel? You might be surprised. The soft pads stick to **surfaces**, but they are not wet.

So how does a gecko hang on to a smooth, slippery surface such as a window? Scientists have figured it out. When a gecko climbs a surface, the tiny hairs on the gecko's toes suddenly stick. They stick because **molecules** in the branching tips get pulled toward the surface. The pull lets a gecko's toes stick like glue to anything!

The force holding the hair tips to a surface is strong. But when a gecko lifts its foot, the pull is broken. The tips let go, and the gecko moves on.

Let go! **A gecko curls up its toes before moving its foot.**

A closer look! **The toe pads of most geckos are covered with millions of hairs that branch at their tips.**

branching tips

Connect Skills to Strategies

How do a lot of tiny branching tips help something stick to a surface? To answer this question, **draw a conclusion**. Use clues in the text and photos, and what you already know.

Now ask and answer your own questions about geckos. Then explain how **asking questions** as you read can help you draw conclusions.

Copying Mother Nature

Scientists have been studying gecko toe hairs. They've been trying to create **artificial** substances that stick to surfaces in the same way. Scientists want to make materials that are dry but can stick to things, just like the gecko toe hairs.

One team has invented a sticky tape made of tiny, plastic **fibers**. The fibers look a lot like the endings of gecko toe hairs. The tape has about 42 million fibers per square centimeter (0.16 square inch). Each fiber is one hundred times smaller than the thickness of a human hair.

When the tape slides across a surface, the fibers stick. When the tape is lifted slightly, the fibers let go. Only a little dirt from the surface sticks to the tape. And the dirt that does stick comes off easily. So the tape can be used again and again.

Which is which?
Scientists copied the shape and size of gecko toe hair endings (left) to make a material (right) that sticks in the same way.

Scientists think that their tape will have many uses. For example, it could help robots move in new ways. With the tape on its feet, a small robot could walk up walls!

You might be using things made with these dry sticky fibers soon, too! Think about a magnet made with tiny hairs like those of gecko feet. You could stick the magnet on a mirror, a window, or just about anywhere.

Put It All Together

Geckos can hang on to almost any surface using their amazing toes. Scientists have figured out the secret of gecko toes. The sticking power comes from how the tiny hairs on their toes act. Scientists are using what they've learned to make new kinds of dry, sticky materials.

Connect Skills to Your Life

Tell how **drawing conclusions** can help you

- understand how things stick to surfaces.
- connect what you're reading to what you already know.
- apply what you know to new situations.

Respond and Go Beyond

Share Ideas After Reading

How could sticky toes help an animal get around? Share what you learned with a partner.

Connect Skills to *The Sticky Secret of Gecko Toes*

Use a Chart to Draw Conclusions

Create a graphic organizer like this chart. Ask questions about geckos and how they move. Then complete the chart, and draw conclusions to answer your questions. Talk about your chart with a partner.

Use the Strategy Go back, reread the text, and think of questions for the graphic organizer.

My Question	Clues in the Text	What I Already Know	My Conclusion
Why can't geckos blink?			

Write About It!

Be a reporter for a science journal.
- Tell about how scientists invented a new dry but sticky tape.
- Draw conclusions about how this tape might be useful at school or at home.

Stretch Your Brain

Walk Up Walls!

Design a pair of shoes that stick like a gecko's toes. Draw a picture of the shoes. Then write a story about what happens the first time you wear your "super sticky" footwear. Share your work with a partner.